ELIZABETH
& PHILIP

AND THEIR ROYAL FAMILY

ELIZABETH & PHILIP

AND THEIR ROYAL FAMILY

Photographs by the
Daily Mail

ATLANTIC WORLD

Queen Elizabeth II is the most popular and successful monarch in British history and at her side, since their wedding in 1947, has been her husband, Prince Philip. This book portrays the extraordinary life of this remarkable woman, her long and successful marriage to the Duke of Edinburgh, and their family – much loved by the British nation, the Commonwealth and the world at large. The enormous zeal she sustains for the state and public occasions she attends, the moments of privacy she shares with her family and her ability to make every occasion special for those that meet her in Britain and around the world set her apart as a monarch who combines the traditional role of royalty while adapting to the needs and expectations of the modern era.

Elizabeth was only twenty-five years old when she pledged her life to the service of her people. This book, beautifully illustrated with photographs from the archives of the *Daily Mail*, shows the undoubted fulfilment of that pledge.

A Royal Dynasty

Two unexpected twists of fate in succeeding generations brought Queen Elizabeth II to the British throne in 1952. The Queen's grandfather, King George V, only became King because of the sudden death from pneumonia of his older brother Prince Albert who was first in line. George married his brother's former fiancée, who became known as Queen Mary, and the couple had five sons and a daughter – Edward, Albert, Mary, Henry, George and John.

Prince Albert, Queen Elizabeth's father, was also second in line to the throne, after his older brother Edward. Albert was created Duke of York in 1920 and, like his father before him, did not anticipate that he would become King. Albert served in the Forces and carried out royal engagements but remained in the background, while Edward was groomed to be King from an early age. Albert had set his heart on marrying Lady Elizabeth Bowes-Lyon but at first she was reluctant to take on the rigours of royal life. She finally accepted his proposal and they were married at Westminster Abbey on 26 April 1923 (left).

Above left: King George V and Queen Mary.

Below and opposite: The newly-married Duke and Duchess of York spend their honeymoon at Polesden Lacey, Surrey, before travelling to Glamis Castle in Scotland.

'You are indeed a lucky man to have such a charming and delightful wife as Elizabeth. I trust you have many years of happiness'.   King George writing to his second son

Royal Families

Opposite above: The Duke and Duchess of York visit Millwall Docks. The couple lived quietly in London and the Duchess regularly supported her husband on royal engagements. The Duke had always been very shy, unlike his socialite older brother, and found these duties very difficult as he also had a pronounced stammer, which hindered public speaking. After he stumbled through his speech to close the British Empire Exhibition, Elizabeth contacted the Australian speech therapist Lionel Logue and helped Albert through the programme devised for him, now portrayed in the film *The King's Speech*.

Opposite below right: During a visit to New Zealand in 1927, the Duchess is able to spend some time fishing.

Opposite below left: Queen Mary and her son Prince George, the Duke of Kent, visit the British Empire Exhibition in 1924.

Above: Prince Andrew of Greece and Denmark pictured with his wife Princess Alice of Battenberg, grand-daughter of Queen Victoria. These were the parents of Queen Elizabeth II's future consort Philip Mountbatten, born 10 June 1921, the youngest of the couple's five children.

Right: Philip as a toddler c. 1922. Around this time, the King of Greece, Philip's uncle, was forced to abdicate while Prince Andrew and his family were banished for life, initially taking up residence in Paris. Although born in Corfu, Philip had little knowledge of the country or language of his birth.

Princess Elizabeth

Opposite: The Duchess of York gave birth to Elizabeth Alexandra Mary on 21 April 1926 at her parents' home in Bruton Street, Mayfair. The new arrival was styled Her Royal Highness Princess Elizabeth, but as third in line to the throne, behind her uncle and father, was never expected to become a monarch. Here the Duchess clutches a teddy bear for her daughter.

Above left: Elizabeth aged two. During her early years the family lived in their private home at 145 Piccadilly, in London; she was cared for by her nanny, Clara 'Allah' Knight who had looked after the Duchess of York as a child.

Above right: On 21 August 1930 the Duke and Duchess's second daughter, Princess Margaret Rose, was born at Glamis Castle.

Left: The Duke with his father at Balmoral. The King was beginning to have major health problems. He suffered from pleurisy and chronic obstructive pulmonary disease and contracted septicaemia in 1928, never making a complete recovery.

At the time of the birth of the King's first grandchild in the male line, Elizabeth Alexandra Mary, on 21 April 1926, no one imagined she would one day inherit the throne.

The King had become a focus of stability and reliability in a darkening decade.

Elizabeth and her Grandpa England

Opposite above: The two young princesses often accompanied their parents on the official engagements expected of the royal family and on this occasion Princess Elizabeth joined the Queen, the Princess Royal, and the Duchess of York to watch the Trooping the Colour ceremony at Horse Guards Parade.

Opposite below right: The Duchess of York takes her two daughters for a day out at the Abergeldie Castle Fete.

Opposite below left: Princess Elizabeth walks through Hyde Park with a friend.

Above: The King and Queen are accompanied by the Duchess of York when they visit Southampton to open the world's largest dry dock.

Left: Princess Elizabeth with her grandparents, King George and Queen Mary. The King adored his granddaughter and she used to call him 'Grandpa England'.

The final decline in the King's health began soon after the Silver Jubilee celebrations in 1935. He was too frail to attend the service of remembrance at the Cenotaph later that year, although he did make his live Christmas broadcast.

Silver Jubilee

Left: In 1935 King George V commemorated his Silver Jubilee. The country celebrated and a Service of Thanksgiving was held at St Paul's Cathedral. Here the King meets one of his admirals aboard the Royal Yacht *Britannia*.

Above: The Duke and Duchess of York, the Duke and Duchess of Kent and the two young princesses leave St Paul's Cathedral, following the service.

Preparing for the Stage

Right: Prince Philip of Greece costumed for the Gordonstoun School's production of *Macbeth*, in Scotland, July 1935. Philip's education reflected the turmoil of Europe. After some years at the American school in Paris, he moved to a private school in England. In 1930 Philip's mother was diagnosed with schizophrenia and hospitalised and his father moved to Monte Carlo, leaving Philip to be brought up and educated under the influence of the Mounbattens, descendants of his maternal grandparents who had rescinded their German titles and taken an English name and nationality during the First World War. He arrived at Gordonstoun School with its founder, Kurt Hahn, the Jewish principal of Schule Schloss Salem who fled Nazi Germany in the early 1930s, forced to abandon the school he had founded and where Philip had recently taken up his studies. Philip completed his school education in 1939 to join the Royal Navy, where he served with distinction through the Second World War.

Opposite above: Crowds gather along Victoria Embankment, London, to see the royal family pass by in their carriages during the Jubilee celebrations. The King also celebrated his 70th birthday that year.

Above left: The Duchess of York makes her first airline journey when the couple visit Brussels. Prince Albert already held a pilot's licence, which he had gained while serving with the Royal Air Force.

Left: In July 1935 the young princesses are taken to the Royal Opera House to watch the Children's Matinée of Ballet. From an early age Princess Margaret showed a love of theatre and the arts.

Above: A few days after her tenth birthday Princess Elizabeth is out in Windsor Park with her riding master Mr Henry Owen. In contrast to her sister, Elizabeth showed a natural love of horses and dogs.

The Death of King George V

King George V's health continued to decline and on 20 January 1936, he passed away at Sandringham House. Edward's accession to the throne was announced immediately after his father's death.

Right: The King's body is brought from Sandringham to London, and his coffin carried from the train at King's Cross to be taken to Westminster Hall for the official lying-in-state. The night before the funeral, his four surviving sons, Edward, Albert, Henry and George, mounted the Vigil of the Princes at the four corners of the catafalque.

Opposite above: (l to r) Prince George; King Edward VIII; Prince Albert and Prince Henry. Their brother John had died at the age of 13 after an epileptic seizure.

Opposite below: Formal curtsies and handshakes at a tree-planting ceremony at Windsor Great Park. Although the girls regularly accompanied their parents, they were usually left behind on foreign tours, as it was believed they were too young to take part. In keeping with tradition the two sisters were educated at home and taught the necessary skills for a royal life.

Below: The young princesses enjoy meeting members of the Royal Company of Archers.

Just before midnight on 20 January 1936, at Sandringham, the King died in the presence of his wife and children. He was seventy years old.

Abdication Crisis

Left: King Edward VIII makes his first radio broadcast to the nation from Broadcasting House in March 1936, shortly after being proclaimed King. Princess Elizabeth was now second in line to the throne but it was fully expected that Edward VIII would marry and have children.

Inset: However, only a few months after his accession, Edward's romance with Mrs Wallis Simpson became the subject of much speculation and it was soon clear that he intended to marry her. This caused a constitutional crisis, as the British monarch is the Supreme Governor of the Church of England and therefore could not marry a divorcée. In December 1936, Edward finally announced his intention to abdicate in a speech from Windsor Castle and the Duke of York became King.

Opposite: Wallis Simpson marries Edward at the Château de Candé in France, 3 June 1937.

Below: Following the marriage, Albert conferred a new title, Duke of Windsor, on his brother. Wallis Simpson became Duchess of Windsor but was never granted permission to use the title Royal Highness, unlike her husband.

Wallis Simpson was the person who was not only to alter the King's entire life but to bring an undreamed of crisis in the history of the British monarchy.

George VI is Crowned

Top: Prince Albert is crowned George VI at Westminster Abbey on 12 May 1937, the date originally planned for Edward's coronation. Albert had been suddenly thrust into this role and was very reluctant to take the crown but had a strong sense of duty and chose the regnal name George to provide greater confidence and continuity for the monarchy.

Opposite top: Queen Elizabeth, now his queen consort, waves to the crowds with Princess Elizabeth from the balcony of Buckingham Palace. Suddenly, at the age of eleven, the princess was now the heir presumptive and her life was about to become very different. Everything was to alter radically as the family moved into the official royal residences and her parents' roles changed.

Britain Prepares for War

Below: The King and Queen return from a very successful visit to the United States and Canada in 1939, and are re-united with their daughters.

Opposite below left: The first few years of the King's reign were dominated by the threat of war. In September 1939 formal photographs of the King and Queen were taken just after his broadcast declaring that Britain was at war with Germany.

Opposite below right: Two months later, the Queen also makes a broadcast to the nation, this time to reassure the mothers of evacuated children.

Bottom: The princesses enjoy a carriage ride with one of the family corgis. The princesses spent most of the war in the relative safety of Windsor Castle.

Wartime Duties

As a gesture of solidarity with the people of London, the King and Queen continued to reside at Buckingham Palace throughout the war, where they were also the target of German bombing raids during the Blitz.

Opposite above left and below: The King and Queen survey the damage to Buckingham Palace following an air raid on the night of 13 September 1940, which destroyed the chapel building.

Right: The Queen joins the King and Prime Minister Winston Churchill to speak to the workers drafted in to clear the damage from bombing.

Opposite above right: Afterwards the Queen makes a visit to the East End of London, to speak to the women and children also affected by the Blitz.

Opposite below: Amid the debris from a bombed London hospital, the Queen pays tribute to the hospital workers, some of whom had been bombed out of their homes and yet continued to work long shifts on the wards. In August 1942 Prince George, the King's brother, was killed when a Short Sunderland flying boat crashed in Scotland in bad weather.

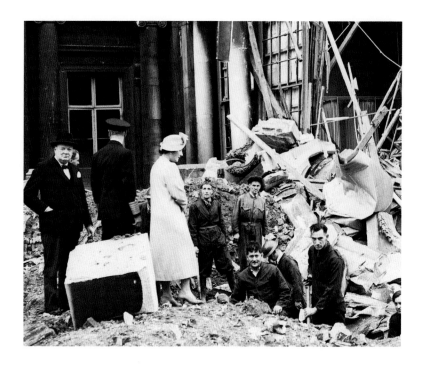

Buckingham Palace was hit nine times in the war, mostly during the heavy bombing of 1940-41. Having had her own home bombed, the Queen felt she could 'look the blitzed East End in the face'.

Throughout Britain's greatest trial, the King and Queen proved to be leaders with identity and purpose, consoling and inspiring a nation under siege. Having reached the age of 18, Princess Elizabeth was allowed to join the ATS, where she became a junior officer.

Joining the War Effort

Opposite above: As the war rumbled on, the British public increasingly took up the 'Dig for Victory' campaign, turning over large areas of land to cultivate crops to feed the populace. The royal family demonstrate their support, joining those harvesting crops grown at Sandringham.

Opposite below: In a bid to save fuel while inspecting the Sandringham House harvest, the King and princesses travel by bicycle, and the Queen makes use of a pony and trap.

Above: In July 1944 Queen Elizabeth and Princess Elizabeth visit a Bomber Command operational station with the King.

Inset: The teenage princesses gather crops in August 1943. At the age of fourteen Princess Elizabeth made her first radio broadcast, on BBC's *Children's Hour*, to the children who had been evacuated during the war.

Left: Princess Elizabeth makes a return visit to the Motor Transport Training Centre at Camberley in Surrey, where she had trained as a driver and a mechanic. Here she inspects and takes the Salute of her former Auxiliary Territorial Service companions, wearing the recently-earned uniform of Junior Commander.

Princess Elizabeth and Prince Philip of Greece, who served with distinction during the war, had kept in touch since meeting at Dartmouth College in 1939.

Elizabeth Comes of Age

Middle right: In January 1947 Princesses Elizabeth and Margaret joined their parents for their first foreign tour when they went to South Africa. While there the princesses take the opportunity to canter along the beach in East London, on the Eastern Cape.

Above right: Princess Elizabeth makes her twenty-first birthday speech to the British Commonwealth from Cape Town in South Africa.

Above left: The princesses pass St Paul's Cathedral on their return to Buckingham Palace after a lunch at the Guildhall with the Lord Mayor.

Below right: The Queen accompanied by her daughters visits the Welsh Corgi Show at Lime Grove Baths in Shepherd's Bush. The King had bought his first corgi named Dookie in 1933 and Princess Elizabeth was given her own corgi for her eighteenth birthday, choosing to call her Susan.

Opposite: The engagement of Princess Elizabeth and Lieutenant Philip Mountbatten was announced on 9 July 1947. He had asked her father for her hand-in-marriage the previous year, but it was agreed to wait until after her twenty-first birthday to formally announce their betrothal.

The day before the wedding the bride's father created his soon to be son-in-law Duke of Edinburgh and with it the authority to use the title 'His Royal Highness'.

Princess Elizabeth Marries

Opposite above: Two years after the end of the war, the royal family and the nation celebrated, as Princess Elizabeth married Lieutenant Philip Mountbatten, nephew of Earl Louis Mountbatten, on 20 November 1947. Although born in Greece, Philip's British citizenship was guaranteed by his career in the Royal Navy during the war; in marrying Elizabeth he renounced his Greek Orthodox religion and received the title Prince Philip, Duke of Edinburgh.

Opposite below: Princess Elizabeth is escorted by the Household Cavalry to Westminster Abbey, in the Irish State Coach. She wore a Norman Hartnell gown but had still needed to save her ration coupons to purchase the material.

Top: The newly-weds wave to the crowds gathered below, accompanied by the King and Queen and bridesmaids Princess Margaret and Lady Mary Cambridge.

Right and inset: After the ceremony they travelled to Lord Mountbatten's Romsey estate, Broadlands, to enjoy their honeymoon.

Welcome Prince Charles

Opposite: Princess Elizabeth gave birth to their first child, Charles Philip Arthur George, on 14 November 1948. His christening took place at Buckingham Palace the following month.

Below left: The young Prince Charles is taken for a walk by his nanny, Mabel Anderson.

Above right: Princess Elizabeth and Princess Margaret leave St Margaret's in Westminster in February 1948 after attending the wedding of the Honourable Sara Ismay to Flight Lieutenant the Honourable Wentworth Beaumont. The groom was aide-de-camp to Earl Mountbatten, Prince Philip's uncle.

Below right: Showing that even the Princesses were affected by post-war austerity, Princesses Elizabeth and Margaret attend the unveiling of the memorial in Grosvenor Square to former US President Franklin D. Roosevelt in their wedding outfits. The memorial, sculpted by Sir William Reid Dick, was unveiled by Roosevelt's wife Eleanor and the assembled audience included Sir Winston Churchill and Prime Minister Clement Attlee.

In November 1948, the King and Queen became grandparents. Prince Charles was born at Buckingham Palace, assuring the succession to a second generation.

Scottish Holidays

Left: While in Scotland the royal family, including the King and Queen, the Marquess of Aberdeen, the Duke and Duchess of Gloucester, the Duke of Edinburgh, Princess Margaret and Princess Elizabeth, attend the Braemar Games.

Centre left: King George VI with Princess Elizabeth and Prince Charles at Ballater Station.

Below: The King and Queen at the Royal Garden Party at Buckingham Palace.

Opposite inset: The King, Queen and Princess Margaret visit children at the Northern Infirmary in Inverness, Scotland. By now the King was beginning to have major problems with his own health. Always a heavy smoker, he developed arteriosclerosis and needed an operation in March 1949 to remove a blockage from the artery in his right leg.

Opposite above left: With his health failing, Princess Elizabeth takes the King's place during the Trooping the Colour ceremony in 1949.

Opposite above right: During a royal visit to the island of Sark, Princess Elizabeth is unexpectedly joined by a terrier named Pip as she listens to an address.

Opposite below: The Queen and various members of the royal family on the balcony of Buckingham Palace after the Trooping the Colour ceremony in 1951. In September the King had a further operation to remove a lung after a malignant tumour was discovered.

It was difficult for Princess Elizabeth to enjoy her life fully as wife of a naval officer and mother. Increasingly she was needed by her parents and to appear on state occasions as concerns over her father's health grew.

An Addition to the Family

Right and above: Three generations are together in the grounds of Balmoral. Princess Anne, born on 15 August 1950, clearly wants to avoid the water in the pond while Prince Charles is keen to investigate. Princess Margaret had recently celebrated her twenty-first birthday.

Left: The Queen and Princess Elizabeth attend the wedding of Lady Caroline Montagu-Douglas-Scott and Mr Ian Hedworth at Westminster Abbey in July 1951.

Queen Elizabeth II

Opposite: On 6 February 1952 King George VI died in his sleep after a long struggle with illness. The nation mourned his loss, but prepared to welcome Princess Elizabeth as Queen Elizabeth II. Here she takes the salute at the Trooping the Colour ceremony in June.

Left: The former Queen, now the Queen Mother, rides in a carriage with Princess Margaret, both dressed in black, at the Trooping the Colour.

Below left: The young Queen makes her way to the French Embassy for a dinner engagement.

Below right: Elizabeth visits the Royal College of Music in London.

On 6 February 1952, Princess Elizabeth, the heir to the throne, and her husband were in Kenya, four thousand miles from home. Their tour had scarcely begun. On that day she ceased to be Princess Elizabeth and became the sixth Queen Regnant in the history of the realm.

Private and Public Events

Opposite above left: Elizabeth and Princess Margaret attend the State Opening of Parliament.

Opposite above right: Elizabeth and Margaret play with Princess Anne at Balmoral Castle.

Opposite below: Elizabeth and Prince Philip with their children, Charles and Anne, at their Clarence House home in London.

Left: The whole family turns out for a garden party at Buckingham Palace. However, in March 1953 Queen Mary, pictured here behind the King, died from lung cancer at the age of eighty-five.

Below: In September 1952, Queen Elizabeth II and Prince Philip are joined at Balmoral Castle by King Faisal and the Regent of Iraq. Princess Anne is just over two years old.

Queen Elizabeth II is Crowned

Elizabeth was crowned on 2 June 1953 at Westminster Abbey. The service was conducted by the Archbishop of Canterbury, Dr Geoffrey Fisher, with 8,000 guests in attendance. An estimated three million people crowded the streets while for many at home, it was their first opportunity to watch television.

Right: Wearing a simple white linen robe known as the Colobium Sindonis, which covers her coronation gown, the Queen is seated in St Edward's Chair.

Opposite above right: Her coronation gown, designed by Norman Hartnell, was embroidered with emblems that represented the United Kingdom and the Commonwealth.

Opposite above left: The Archbishop of Canterbury raises the St Edward's Crown. As soon as the crown was placed on her head the crowds shouted 'God Save the Queen' and a 21-gun salute was fired at the Tower of London.

Below: After the ceremony, the newly crowned Queen Elizabeth II leaves the Abbey.

Opposite below right: On her return to Buckingham Palace the Queen appears on the balcony to greet the crowds below and to watch the traditional flypast salute. She appeared again at 9.45pm to turn on the 'Lights of London'.

The Queen went through the
three-hour ritual, its form a
thousand years old, flawlessly.
The weather was cold but still
millions of people lined the
processional streets.

A Mother and Now a Queen

Opposite above left: Prince Charles and Princess Anne join their grandmother on the balcony to watch the flypast on the Queen's official birthday.

Opposite below left: The Queen and Princess Anne, with her pony Greensleeves, during their summer holiday at Balmoral in 1955.

Opposite below right: Queen Elizabeth attends the 1955 Royal Variety Show at the Victoria Palace Theatre.

Opposite above right: Her Majesty arrives at Westminster Abbey, cloaked in white mink, for the Order of the Bath ceremony in 1956.

Above: During the Trooping the Colour ceremony in 1954 the crowds were keen to sing to the Duke of Edinburgh as he was celebrating his 33rd birthday.

Right: Lord Mountbatten accompanies the Queen to the premiere of Leslie Norman's *Dunkirk* in March 1958. John Mills led the cast as Corporal 'Tubby' Binns.

Elizabeth witnessed the ongoing transformation of the British Empire into the Commonwealth of Nations. Spanning 1953–54, the Queen and her husband embarked on a six-month around-the-world tour. She became the first reigning monarch of Australia and New Zealand to visit those nations. She is the most widely travelled head of state in history.

Princess Margaret Marries

Right: Wearing a silk organza Norman Hartnell gown, Princess Margaret arrives at Westminster Abbey for her marriage to photographer Antony Armstrong-Jones. After the ceremony in May 1960, the title of Earl of Snowdon was bestowed on Armstrong-Jones.

Opposite above left: The bride was given away by her brother-in-law the Duke of Edinburgh and it was the duty of the ten-year-old Princess Anne to lead the eight bridesmaids down the aisle. With the celebrations over, the happy couple are given a rose petal send-off, before embarking on their honeymoon on the Royal Yacht.

Opposite above right: The Queen attends a dinner held at the American Embassy in London, hosted by the American Vice-President, Richard Nixon.

Below: On 19 February 1960, the Queen gave birth to her third child and second son, Andrew. Here she spends time with her husband, three children, and one of her beloved corgis, at Balmoral.

Opposite below: The Queen Mother spends her sixtieth birthday at Clarence House in the company of her three grandchildren. In March she distributed the Maundy Money at Westminster Abbey for the first time, standing in for her daughter after Prince Andrew's birth.

Margaret had taken care to conceal her romance from reporters. The ceremony was the first royal wedding to be broadcast on television, and attracted viewing figures of 300 million worldwide.

A Remarkable Woman

Left: The Duke of Edinburgh attends a wedding in Germany, accompanied by his mother in 1957. Despite many personal difficulties, including congenital deafness and diagnosed schizophrenia, Philip's mother was an extraordinary woman; she showed heroism in World War II, remaining in Athens during the Nazi occupation and aiding a Jewish family to evade the death camps. In 1949 she founded a nursing order of the Greek Orthodox Church and thereafter adopted the attire of a nun, travelling to the USA on fund-raising tours. A surprisingly satisfying turn of events came about when in 1967, her health failing, she was invited to live at Buckingham Palace for the remaining two years of her colourful life; having been born in one Royal Palace – Windsor Castle – she ended her days in another in 1969. Following her wishes she was buried on the Mount of Olives in Jerusalem.

Below left: The Queen and Prince Charles await the arrival of the Duke of Edinburgh at London Airport.

Below right: The Queen arrives for the royal premiere of the comedy *Man in the Moon*.

Opposite below: The Queen visits the newly-restored Palm House at the Royal Botanical Gardens in Kew, as part of its bicentennial celebrations.

The Duke's Award

Above and opposite below centre: A chance to relax in the grounds of Windsor Castle in 1959, shortly before embarking on a tour of North America. The smiling couple seem to carry the burden of royalty with ease, belying their wider responsibilities.

In 1956 the Duke of Edinburgh Award was announced as a pilot programme to give young men and women a 'sense of responsibility to themselves and their communities'. The idea originated from a scheme created by the innovative headmaster of Gordonstoun School; the Duke was the nominal head and chair but Sir John Hunt, whose expedition first conquered Mt Everest in 1953 was the first administrator of the scheme and was responsible for much of its initial design. The Award, formally founded as a charity in 1959, proved popular from the start and has grown from its initial enrolment of 7,000 to a current annual participation of over 300,000 in the UK. Having spread to over 140 territories around the world the scheme has had a profound effect on over eight million young people.

A Busy Diary

Opposite above right: In March 1961 the Queen and the Duke of Edinburgh visited Nepal. The same year, the Duke became the first president of the newly founded World Wildlife Fund, UK, a position he held for 20 years, followed by his presidency of WWF International until 1996.

Opposite above left: The Queen arrives for the screening of *The Guns of Navarone* in May 1961.

Opposite below left: The Queen greets the new President of the United States of America, John F. Kennedy and his wife, Jackie, at an official reception at Buckingham Palace.

Opposite below right: Prior to the start of the official racing at Royal Ascot it was customary for members of the Royal Family to race against each other in the morning. The Queen can be seen finishing in sixth place. Princess Alexandra came in first on this occasion.

Above left: The Queen presents the Wimbledon Championship Trophy to Australia's Rod Laver in 1962.

Above right: The Queen and the Duke of Edinburgh attend the annual service in the chapel at St Paul's Cathedral for the Orders of St Michael and St George.

Left: The Queen's cousin, the Duke of Kent, escorts his bride Miss Katharine Worsley, down the aisle of York Minster.

Prince Andrew, arrived in 1960 while Edward was born at Buckingham Palace in March 1964. They were the first children to be born to a reigning monarch since Queen Victoria had her family.

A Third Son for the Queen

Opposite above and below: On 10 March 1964, the Queen gave birth to her fourth child, Prince Edward, at Buckingham Palace. The Queen and her family, including baby Edward, are pictured together at Frogmore, Windsor, on her thirty-ninth birthday.

Above left: A young Prince Andrew joins his mother on the balcony at Buckingham Palace after the Trooping the Colour ceremony in 1962.

Above: The Queen attends the gala performance of *Tosca* at Covent Garden in July 1965.

Middle left: In the same month, Elizabeth II becomes the first reigning monarch since 1671 to make an official visit to the Isle of Wight.

Below left: Ken Dodd, Dudley Moore, Spike Milligan and Max Bygraves are introduced to the Queen at the Royal Variety Show held at the London Palladium.

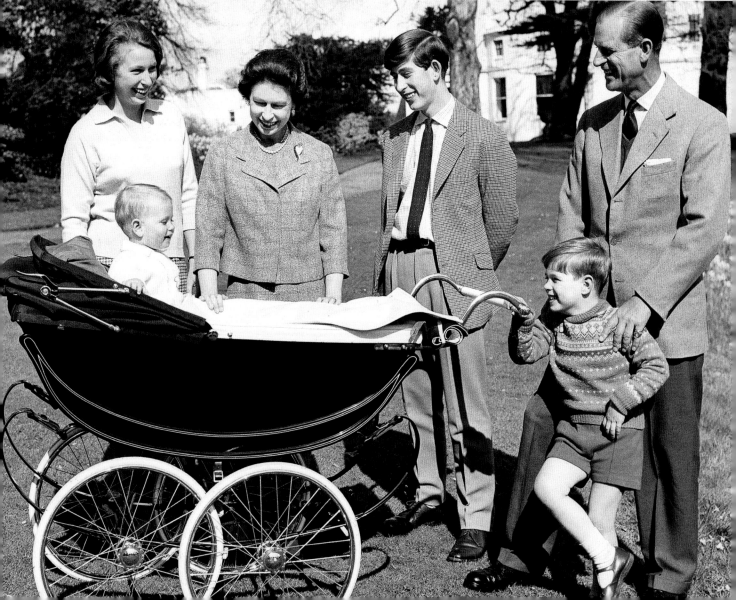

Welcoming the President

Above: A month after his inauguration in January 1969, Richard Nixon, President of the United States, joins the Queen and the Duke of Edinburgh for lunch at Buckingham Palace.

Left: On 7 March 1969, after unveiling a plaque at Victoria Station to formally open the new Victoria Underground Line, the Queen takes a ride to Green Park. The cost of the ticket was 5d.

Opposite above left: The Queen leads the Trooping the Colour ceremony in 1967.

Opposite below left: An opportunity to spend her forty-second birthday at Windsor Castle with the whole family.

Opposite below right: After a recent visit to South America the Queen attends a service at St George's Chapel Windsor. The Dean of Windsor, the Very Reverend John Woods is there to greet her.

Opposite above right: William Dix, who played the character Tommy Stubbins, is introduced to the Queen at the premiere of *Doctor Doolittle*. Joan Collins, the wife of co-star Anthony Newley, stands alongside.

Prince Charles was created Prince of Wales on 26 July 1958, though his actual investiture did not take place until 1 July 1969. He spent ten weeks leading up to his Investiture learning about Welsh culture and language and during the ceremony he gave his replies in both English and Welsh.

Charles, Prince of Wales

Above: Prince Charles sits with his mother and father on the Royal Dais at Caernarvon Castle in North Wales during his investiture as the Prince of Wales in July 1969. The tradition of investing the heir to the throne with this title dates back to Edward I in 1301 when he bestowed the honour upon his son after conquering Wales. The ceremony was watched by millions but created hostility among Welsh Nationalists. The day before the Inauguration, two men were killed attempting to plant a bomb outside the government offices at Abergele.

Right: Castle cannons hold more appeal for five-year-old Prince Edward.

Opposite above: The Queen Mother takes her grandson's arm after leaving a church service with other members of the family.

Opposite below: The Prince of Wales joins his parents for the Twenty-fifth Anniversary Variety Performance, held in aid of the Army Benevolent Fund.

Family Celebrations

Above left: Prince Edward and his cousins Lady Sarah and Viscount Linley join their grandmother for her 70th birthday at Clarence House in August 1970.

Above right: Prince Edward accompanies his mother to Badminton in April 1971. He was initially educated by a governess at Buckingham Palace but began formal schooling at the age of seven.

Right: The Queen emerges from King Edward VII Hospital in Marylebone after visiting her daughter. Princess Anne was admitted for an emergency operation to remove an inflamed ovarian cyst.

Opposite above left: On her 21st birthday Princess Anne, accompanied by other members of the family, disembarks from the Royal Yacht *Britannia* in Thurso, Scotland. It proved to be a very successful year for her equestrian career as she won the European Eventing Championship and was voted BBC Sports Personality of the Year in December.

Opposite above right: The royal family leave St George's Chapel, Windsor, on Christmas Day 1971.

Opposite middle right: The Queen studies the mask of Tutankhamun after formally opening the exhibition at the British Museum on 30 March 1972. Running for nine months the 'Treasures of Tutankhamun' attracted nearly 1.7 million visitors with many queueing for up to eight hours to see the priceless collection.

Opposite below right: A chance to visit St Peter's Church of England School in London, which was celebrating its centenary.

Opposite below left: The Queen pictured at the American Friends' gala performance of *The Sleeping Beauty*.

> *'It is a complete misconception to imagine that the monarchy exists in the interests of the monarch. It doesn't. It exists in the interests of the people'.*
>
> Prince Philip, Duke of Edinburgh

Silver Wedding Anniversary

Opposite: The Queen and Prince Philip celebrated their silver wedding anniversary in 1972. A series of photographs was commissioned to mark the event.

Top: Politically and economically, 1972 was important as the year in which Britain entered the Common Market. In the following January, the Queen and Prince Philip attended the official 'Fanfare for Europe' Gala at Covent Garden to celebrate the event. The Queen arrives with Edward Heath, the Prime Minister.

Above inset: The New London Bridge, stretching between the City of London and Southwark, was officially opened by the Queen on 17 March 1973. After the glittering ceremony she is able to meet the waiting children while on her walkabout.

Right: The Queen goes about her work at Balmoral.

Princess Anne Weds

Above left: Princess Anne married Lieutenant Mark Phillips at Westminster Abbey on 14 November 1973. After the ceremony they greet well-wishers from the balcony at Buckingham Palace.

Above right: The Queen is pictured on her forty-eighth birthday.

Left: The Queen visits Aberfan Cemetery in Wales, to lay a wreath at the slate memorial cross, which commemorates the loss of the 116 children and 28 adults who perished in 1966 in the Aberfan disaster. The village school was buried beneath thousands of tons of coal-waste that collapsed and slid from the hill above.

Opposite above left: Garden flowers are presented to the monarch when she visits the Boys' and Girls' Brigade Headquarters in London.

Opposite above right: The Queen and Prince Philip take some of the younger members of the family to visit the Duke of Beaufort's hounds.

Opposite below: Eric Morecambe and Ernie Wise meet the Queen at the Odeon Leicester Square, when she attends the preview of *Lost Horizon*, starring Sir John Gielgud, Sally Kellerman and Peter Finch.

Official Duties

Opposite above: The Queen is pictured with Her Majesty's bodyguard of the Yeoman of the Guard, following an inspection at Buckingham Palace.

Opposite below left: The English cricket team are introduced to the Queen by their captain Tony Greig as they prepare to begin the Second Test against Australia.

Opposite below right: Laura Gisbourne presents flowers to the Queen at the premiere of *Rooster Cogburn*. Laura's father David had been killed in the Red Lion riots the previous year and the screening was held in aid of the Police Dependants' Trust.

Above left: Prince Charles spends the evening of his twenty-sixth birthday at the Vaudeville Theatre watching Alan Ayckbourn's *Absurd Person Singular*. He is joined by his mother and Princess Alexandra; the Queen's cousin and daughter of the Duke of Kent, who was killed in 1942.

Above right: King Constantine of Greece and Mr John Ambler, the husband of Princess Margaretha of Sweden, join the Queen at the Royal Windsor Horse Show.

Right: An opportunity to look at one of the show gardens at the Chelsea Flower Show.

'When I was twenty-one I pledged my life to the service of our people and I asked for God's help to make good that vow. Although that vow was made in my salad days, when I was green in judgement, I do not regret nor retract one word of it'.

Silver Jubilee 1977

Opposite above: In 1977 the country commemorated the twenty-five-year anniversary of the Queen's accession to the throne. To celebrate the event, she undertook a massive Commonwealth tour taking in thirty-six countries in three months.

Opposite below and inset: The royal family attended a Thanksgiving Service at St Paul's Cathedral, followed by a carriage procession back to the Palace. Thousands of street parties were held as the nation joined in the celebrations. As part of the festivities the Queen lit a bonfire at Windsor Castle, setting up a chain of further beacons throughout the country. On 9 June she travelled by boat along the Thames to open the South Bank Jubilee Gardens and the Silver Jubilee Walkway. The evening culminated in a firework display and a procession of lighted carriages back to Buckingham Palace.

Below right: Thousands lined the streets during the Queen's tour of Brighton. Many of the Jubilee visits focused on schools and were filmed. The footage was later used to make a television programme with Valerie Singleton, the former *Blue Peter* presenter, as host.

Left: Similar scenes were repeated during the monarch's visit to the Channel Islands in 1978.

Below left: The Queen can't conceal her excitement as she watches her horse English Harbour compete in the Derby.

It was Lord Mountbatten who had arranged the visit of King George VI and Queen Elizabeth to Dartmouth Royal Naval College on 22 July 1939, taking care to invite the young Princess Elizabeth. It was there that she would meet her future husband.

Joy and Sorrow

Above: In November 1979 the Queen and Prince Philip celebrated their thirty-second wedding anniversary at Balmoral with their children and their first grandson, two-year-old Peter Phillips.

Middle left: The Queen and Princess Michael of Kent are seated among other spectators at the Badminton Horse Trials.

Below left: The Queen Mother, accompanied by her daughters, waves to the crowds from the balcony at Buckingham Palace in July 1980. She is celebrating her 80th birthday.

Opposite: On 27 August 1979 Lord Mountbatten took some of his family fishing just off the coast of Northern Ireland. An IRA bomb, planted on his boat, *Shadow V*, was detonated while they were all aboard. Mountbatten and his grandson Nicholas Knatchbull were killed along with two others including a young crew member. The funeral was held at Westminster Abbey with all the royal family present.

The Prince of Wales had known Lady Diana for several years, but he first took a serious interest in her as a potential bride during the summer of 1980, when they were guests at a country weekend, where she watched him play polo.

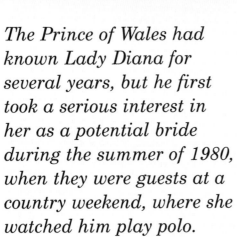

A Royal Engagement

Opposite above left: The paparazzi photograph Lady Diana Spencer outside her London flat in Earls Court. After an initial meeting a few years earlier, a romance between Prince Charles and Lady Diana began to blossom after they spent a weekend together at a country house party. They tried to keep their romance a secret but were soon found out by the press.

Opposite above right: Diana had already shown a natural ability to care for children and worked in a kindergarten and as a part-time nanny.

Below: After a swift courtship, Buckingham Palace announces their engagement on 24 February 1981.

Left: Diana wears her engagement ring, which is similar in style to her mother's with a large sapphire surrounded by a ring of fourteen diamonds.

Opposite below: To keep her away from the watching eyes of the press, Diana moved into Buckingham Palace and soon began to accompany the Prince on official visits. When Charles competed in the Horse and Hound Grand Military Gold Cup at Sandown she was among the spectators, accompanied by Andrew Parker Bowles.

The 'fairytale wedding' was watched by a global television audience of 750 million while 2 million people lined the streets to catch a glimpse of Diana en route to the ceremony.

Charles and Diana

Opposite below: Two million spectators line the streets of London as Diana makes the journey from Clarence House to St Paul's Cathedral in the Glass Coach. The wedding took place on 29 July 1981, with a public holiday declared for the nation.

Opposite above left: Diana's dress, designed by David and Elizabeth Emanuel, had been made by Mrs Nina Missetzis, and included a stunning twenty-five-foot train.

Opposite above right and below right: The newly-weds wave to the crowds as the procession winds its way through the streets back to Buckingham Palace, where the couple appeared to the waiting crowds on the balcony.

Left: After the celebrations and a brief stay at Broadlands, former home of Lord Mountbatten, the couple embarked on a two-week cruise around the Mediterranean on the Royal Yacht *Britannia*, before travelling to Balmoral to join the rest of the royal family for their summer break. While in Scotland they pause for an official photocall.

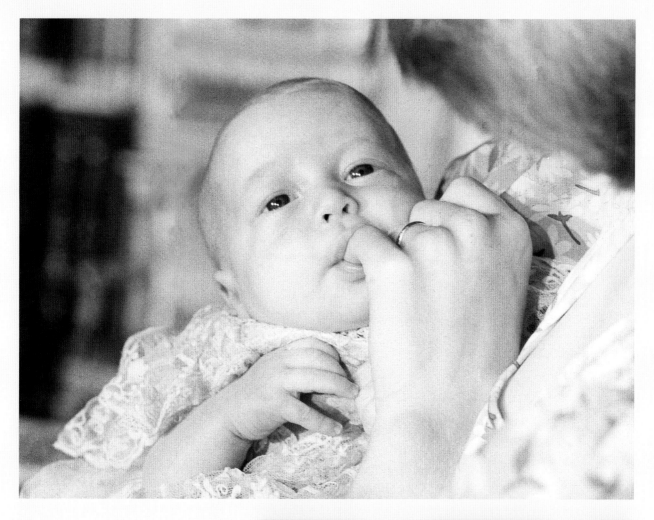

On 5 November 1981, the Princess's first pregnancy was officially announced.

William and Harry

Opposite below left: Prince Charles tentatively holds his new son. On 21 June 1982, just ten days before her twenty-first birthday, Diana gave birth to their first child, Prince William, at the private wing of St Mary's Hospital, London with Charles present throughout the birth.

Opposite above: On 4 August, the young prince, now second in line to the throne, is christened William Arthur Philip Louis at Buckingham Palace.

Above: A comforting finger to settle the prince.

Right: Two years later, on 15 September 1984, the Princess gave birth to their second son, Prince Henry Charles Albert David, to be known as Harry.

Opposite below right: The press gather outside to wait for the royal couple to emerge with their new son.

Business and Pleasure

Opposite above left: Pope John Paul II meets the Queen in her capacity as the Supreme Governor of the Church of England. It was the first time a reigning pope had travelled to Britain. He visited nine cities, delivered sixteen addresses and travelled to Canterbury Cathedral for a joint service with the Archbishop of Canterbury, Dr Robert Runcie.

Opposite above right: The Queen and Prince Philip attend the wedding of Edwina Hicks to Jeremy Brudenell at Christ Church Cathedral in Oxford. The bride was the granddaughter of the Earl of Mountbatten.

Opposite below left: The Queen and Prince Philip inspect the course for the Norwich Union Horse Driving Trials.

Opposite below right: A chance for the Queen to watch her husband take part in the four-in-hand driving at Windsor Horse Show.

Opposite inset: Princess Diana accompanies the Queen to the State Opening of Parliament.

Above right: A moment of chivalry from her son Charles when the Queen watches him play polo at the Guards Polo Club.

Middle right: Princess Anne joins her parents to bid farewell to the President of Mexico and his wife who have just completed a state visit.

Below middle and right: Away from the formalities of royal life, Her Majesty takes the opportunity to walk her corgis along a Norfolk beach during a visit to Sandringham in July 1984.

Below left: At the beginning of 1986 the press picked up the scent of another impending royal engagement and soon began to pursue Sarah Ferguson, who had met Prince Andrew at a party at Windsor Castle the previous year.

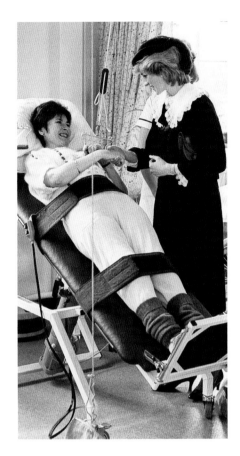

The Queen hosted President Ronald Reagan at Windsor Castle in 1982, and visited his ranch in 1983.

Early in 1982 the Queen was anxious but proud of Prince Andrew who was serving with British forces during the Falklands War.

Andrew and Sarah

Above: Prince Andrew and Sarah Ferguson wave to the crowds after their marriage at Westminster Abbey on 23 July 1987. Their eight attendants include Zara Phillips and Prince William.

Left: The newly-styled Duke and Duchess of York enjoy the racing at Ascot.

Opposite above right: The Queen travels to Croydon to open the new gardens at the Town Hall.

Opposite middle right: The Prince and Princess of Wales in Aberdovey during a Welsh tour. They had recruited the nanny Barbara Barnes to look after their young sons so they could continue their royal engagements. They frequently took their children with them in contrast to Prince Charles who had usually stayed at home with his nanny when his parents were travelling for long periods.

Opposite above left: Diana talks to patients during a visit to the spinal injuries unit in Stanmore. Her compassion for people strongly influenced her work and the charities she supported.

Opposite below: After the Economic Summit in June 1984 a banquet was held at Buckingham Palace. Guests included the US President Ronald Reagan and British Prime Minister Margaret Thatcher.

Princess of Wales

Right: A visit to St Catherine's Hospice in Crawley, Surrey draws in large crowds. Diana's popularity rapidly grew and people flocked to see her.

Below right and opposite below: In March 1988, the Queen and Prince Philip attend the Maundy Service at Lichfield Cathedral, where members of the local community receive the traditional Maundy Money.

Below left: During a visit to the Royal Hospital, Chelsea, the Queen is invited to plant a new lime tree 'Chelsea Sentinel' in the grounds. The original tree, along with around 700 others, had been blown down by the hurricane force winds in October 1987, devastating the arboretum. Horticulturalists had successfully bred new trees from graftings.

Opposite above: Princess Diana is joined by Princess Michael of Kent on the balcony for the parade following the Trooping the Colour ceremony.

Prep School

Below: Prince William begins his last year at Wetherby School. One of the first events in the school calendar is the annual Harvest Festival at St Matthew's Church, Bayswater.

Bottom: William was a keen sportsman from an early age and excelled at football and swimming.

Left: After Wetherby he enrolled at Ludgrove Preparatory School in Berkshire. Headmaster Gerald Barber greets him on his first day in September 1990.

Diana wanted her two sons to have wider experiences than are usual for royal children. She took William and his brother to theme parks and McDonald's; in addition they visited AIDS clinics and shelters for the homeless.

Presidential Visits

Top: US President George Bush and his wife Barbara are invited to Buckingham Palace during a visit to Britain.

Middle left: Former US President Ronald Reagan in the Garden Entrance of Buckingham Palace after the ceremony to appoint him an honorary Knight Grand Cross of the Most Honourable Order of the Bath.

Above: In June 1991 the Queen and Prince Philip join the crowds in the City of London to welcome home over one thousand service men and women who had served in the Gulf War.

Left: The royal family leave church after the traditional Christmas morning service.

Princess Anne Re-marries

Inset: Princess Anne and Royal Navy Commander Timothy Laurence leave Crathie Church after their wedding on 12 December 1992.

Above left: The Queen takes the salute at the Trooping the Colour ceremony.

Above right: The Queen toasts the assembled audience at a lunch at the Guildhall. She had just delivered a speech to celebrate the fortieth year of her accession to the throne and talked also of her 'annus horribilis'. The worry of the breakdown in her children's marriages was added to by the extensive fire at Windsor Castle in November.

Left: Prince William enjoys a skiing holiday in Austria.

Above: Members of the royal family arrive for the marriage of Lady Helen Windsor and art dealer Tim Taylor at St George's Chapel in Windsor.

Middle: The Queen studies some of the exhibits after opening the new £10 million home for the Crown Jewels at the Tower of London. The building contained moving walkways that would allow up to 2,500 visitors an hour to view the priceless collection.

Bottom: A day of frustration for Her Majesty at the Epsom races.

In an unusually personal speech in 1992, following a difficult year for the royal family, Queen Elizabeth said that any institution must expect criticism, but suggested it be done with 'a touch of humour, gentleness and understanding'.

Charles and Diana Separate

Opposite inset: During a visit to India in 1992, Princess Diana is pictured sitting alone in front of the Taj Mahal, the famous monument to love. It soon became clear that the marriage was in trouble and at the end of the year Prime Minister John Major announced the Wales's separation in the House of Commons.

Opposite above right: Always a firm favourite day out, the boys visit Thorpe Park with their mother in 1993.

Opposite below: William and Harry with their grandfather and great-grandmother.

Left and below: Prince William arrives for his first day at Eton College in September 1995. He was soon to excel at sport and left seven years later having gained nine GCSEs and three A levels.

'She proved in the last year that she needed no royal title to continue to generate her particular brand of magic'.

Charles Spencer

Death of Princess Diana

Opposite above left: In 1995, Princess Diana had been awarded the Humanitarian of the Year Award, in recognition of the compassionate work she had undertaken for over 15 years. This continued in 1997 with a campaign against landmines, which saw her travelling to Angola on behalf of the Red Cross and the Halo Trust. The press were there to capture the moment she walked into an area that had been mined.

After her divorce from Prince Charles, Princess Diana began a relationship with Dodi Fayed, son of the millionaire Mohamed Al-Fayed. The couple were constantly followed by the paparazzi and on 31 August 1997, after dinner at the Paris Ritz, the couple were killed in a tunnel after their speeding car was chased by photographers who had discovered their whereabouts.

Top and middle left: After Princess Diana died, the Queen and Prince Philip remained at Balmoral, shielding their grandsons from the press. These days of seclusion caused a public outcry and so the day before the funeral the Queen gave a public address in which she expressed her admiration for Diana and praised Diana's devotion to her sons. The Queen and Prince Philip then went out to meet some of the crowds gathered at the gates of Buckingham Palace and looked at the masses of flowers.

Below: The funeral took place on 6 September at Westminster Abbey. Over a million people lined the route and stood in silence as the cortège passed. After the service the roads back to the Spencer family seat at Althorp were lined with more mourners who threw flowers onto the hearse. She was finally laid to rest on an island in the middle of a lake, in a private ceremony.

Opposite above right: Prince Charles talks quietly to his two sons aged only fifteen and twelve.

Opposite below: Charles, Prince Philip, Prince William, Prince Harry and Earl Spencer, Diana's brother, stand in silence as the coffin is carried past them into the Abbey. They had walked behind Diana's coffin for the entire procession route.

Golden Wedding Anniversary

Above left: As part of the events to mark their Golden Wedding Anniversary the Queen and Prince Philip meet Prime Minister Tony Blair and his wife Cherie before celebrating with a lunch at the Banqueting House in Whitehall.

Middle left: During a three-day state visit to Brunei in September 1998 the Queen speaks at a banquet held in her honour by the Sultan of Brunei, at his palace, the Istana Nurul Iman, in Bandar Seri Begawan.

Below left: The Queen attends the service for the Order of the Bath at Westminster Abbey.

Below right: The Queen stands during a minute's silence at the Arc de Triomphe in Paris during a ceremony to mark the eightieth anniversary of the end of World War I.

Opposite above: Happier times for William and Harry as they fool around with their father during a skiing holiday in Klosters.

Opposite below: Further tomfoolery after Prince William is given his first driving lesson at Highgrove by police driving instructor Sergeant Chris Gilbert in July 1999.

Edward and Sophie

Above: Prince Edward married Sophie Rhys-Jones on 19 June 1999. Breaking with tradition, they chose to have the service at St George's Chapel, Windsor. Afterwards they were given the titles the Earl and Countess of Wessex.

Above left: The Queen chooses lemon when she attends the wedding of HRH Princess Alexia of Greece and Denmark and Carlos Morales Quintana at St Sophia Cathedral in London.

Below left: After visiting Moorfields Eye Hospital in London to help celebrate its centenary Her Majesty meets the crowds waiting outside.

Above right: During a four-day State visit to Italy in October 2000 the Queen was granted an audience with Pope John Paul II at the Vatican in Rome. Dressed in black and wearing a veil, the Queen is welcomed by the eighty-year-old leader of the Roman Catholic Church at the door of his study. They had a private meeting lasting twenty minutes and were able to exchange presents during this time.

The Queen Mother's life spanned one of the most turbulent centuries in history. She lived through war and peace, times of great joy and disaster. She faced every difficult situation with courage that inspired others.

Tearful Times

Below right: The front page of *The Mail on Sunday* on 31 March 2002 pays homage to the Queen Mother, who died in her sleep at her home in the Royal Lodge, at Windsor Great Park with her daughter Queen Elizabeth by her side. She was 101 years old.

Above left: Her great-grandsons follow the gun carriage that carries her coffin from Westminster Hall to Westminster Abbey. At the moment the coffin arrived at the main door, a two-minute silence was held throughout the country. After the service she was laid to rest in St George's Chapel alongside her husband King George VI.

Below left: The front page of the *Daily Mail* on the day of the funeral shows the flag-draped coffin of Queen Elizabeth the Queen Mother. It is guarded at the four corners of the catafalque by her four grandsons: the Duke of York, the Earl of Wessex, Lord Linley and the Prince of Wales, on the eve of her funeral.

Above right: The Queen arrives at Westminster Abbey for the state memorial service for her sister Princess Margaret, who had died in February. Unlike other royal funerals, the Princess's had been a private service conducted at Slough crematorium. Afterwards her ashes were placed in her parents' tomb.

'Everyone is touched by her knowledge, her sensitivity and her incredible sense of humour. You know you are dealing with someone who understands the world and who has a calmness and serenity that are very impressive'.

Kofi Annan

Golden Jubilee

Opposite above left: In June 2002, Queen Elizabeth II celebrated her Golden Jubilee. The event was marked by extensive celebrations, including a Thanksgiving Service at St Paul's Cathedral, a parade and carnival along The Mall, a flypast involving the Red Arrows and Concorde, the Party at the Palace concert at Buckingham Palace and a huge firework display. Here the Queen makes her way to St Paul's in the Gold State Coach, which she had previously used only for her coronation and the Silver Jubilee celebrations.

Opposite above right: Edward and Sophie, the Earl and Countess of Wessex, join the procession to the cathedral in an open-topped coach.

Left and below: Andrew, the Duke of York, shares his carriage with Princes William and Harry and all walk into the Abbey together.

Opposite below: Much merriment as Prince William, Prince Charles and the Queen watch the Jubilee carnival in The Mall.

Royal Carriages

Opposite: Prince Philip at the reins enjoys the sport of carriage driving whose rule book he helped to draft when he took it up after giving up polo in 1971. As well as his enthusiasm for equestrian sport, his naval training found a continuing outlet in yachting: he and the Queen regularly attended Cowes Week in the royal yacht *Britannia*.

Right inset: The Queen leaves Buckingham Palace in a horse-drawn carriage for the State Opening of Parliament in 2002.

Left inset: In June 2003 Princes William and Harry join their grandparents on the balcony to watch the flypast after the annual Trooping the Colour ceremony.

Above left: Queen Elizabeth II and The Duke of Edinburgh attend the service, held every four years, to celebrate the Order of the British Empire at St Paul's Cathedral.

Above right: Her Majesty delivers her speech to the House of Lords during the State Opening of Parliament in 2004.

Below right: With a walking stick for support, the Queen leaves the King Edward VII Hospital in January 2003, after keyhole surgery on her right knee. The injury occurred while she walking on uneven ground during a private visit to Newmarket.

Charles and Camilla

Left: On 9 April 2005, Prince Charles married his long-term companion Camilla Parker Bowles, who was then granted the title, Duchess of Cornwall. The ceremony took place at the Guildhall in Windsor.

Below: Princes Harry and William and Zara and Peter Phillips emerge from St George's Chapel, Windsor, where the marriage had been blessed by the Archbishop of Canterbury, Rowan Williams.

Opposite above left: Prince Charles joins delegates from fifty countries gathered together to celebrate the re-opening of the Old Bridge in Mostar, Bosnia, destroyed in the Bosnian War.

Opposite above right: Prince Charles meets former glider pilots at the Pegasus Bridge Monument to commemorate the sixtieth anniversary of D-Day in June 2004.

Opposite below: Prince Charles and his sons stand in silence as the Queen unveils the Diana Memorial Fountain in Hyde Park.

Opposite centre right: On a happier note, Prince Charles joins Jamelia for the Party in the Park at Hyde Park, held in aid of the Prince's Trust. The singer is an ambassador for the charity and also performed at the concert.

The wedding made Charles the first member of the royal family to have a civil, rather than religious, wedding in England.

Evening Standard

WEST END FINAL

LONDON, FRIDAY, 21 APRIL 2006

SO HAPPY AND GLORIOUS AT 80

Happy 80th Birthday

Opposite below left: The front page of the *Evening Standard* on 21 April 2006 celebrates the Queen's eightieth birthday, picturing the monarch outside Windsor Castle where over 20,000 people had gathered.

Left: Her Majesty enters Westminster Abbey in traditional red and white robes for the Most Honourable Order of the Bath ceremony in May 2006. The ceremony dates back to medieval times and installs new knights into the chivalric order.

Below: Wearing his gown and hood, Prince William holds his certificate after the ceremony awarding him a Master's degree in Geography from the University of St Andrews, Scotland.

Opposite above: With her husband by her side the Duchess of Cornwall undertakes her first official function as she opens a new playground near Balmoral.

Opposite below right: Full ceremonial dress is required for The Order of the Garter ceremony at Windsor Castle.

Diamond Wedding Anniversary

Opposite above: Princes William and Harry arriving at Westminster Abbey with Prince Charles and Camilla, Duchess of Cornwall for a service to celebrate the diamond wedding anniversary of the Queen and Prince Philip.

Opposite below: Queen Elizabeth II and the Duke of Edinburgh with Jacob Zuma, the President of South Africa, and his wife Tobeka Madiba Zuma, during a state banquet at Buckingham Palace.

Right: The Queen and Prince Philip arrive in a traditional carriage for the second day at Royal Ascot in June 2009.

Below: The Queen and Prince Philip leave the Service of Commemoration held at St Paul's Cathedral to mark the end of the hostilities with Iraq.

William and Kate

Left and below left: Prince William and his fiancée Kate Middleton pose for the photographers at St James's Palace after their engagement is announced on 16 November 2010. It was revealed that they had become engaged during a visit to Kenya the previous month. William gave her the sapphire and diamond engagement ring that previously belonged to his mother.

Opposite: William and Kate were married in Westminster Abbey on 29 April 2011. The event was watched by an estimated 2 billion people around the world. Kate's dress, a closely guarded secret, was designed by Sarah Burton at Alexander McQueen. Made of satin, it featured a lace appliqué bodice made at the Royal School of Needlework. The train measured nearly 9 feet and she wore the Cartier scroll tiara lent to her by the Queen. As the bridal procession began the three-and-a-half-minute walk down the aisle, they were watched by their 1,900 guests, while the choir sang an anthem by Sir Hubert Parry. The wedding service was led by the Dean of Westminster, John Hall, assisted by Rowan Williams, Archbishop of Canterbury, and Richard Chartres, the Bishop of London.

Below right: The couple photographed during Kate's first formal royal engagement in February 2011.

Newly-weds

Opposite below: Kate and William make their journey through the streets of London in a 1902 State Landau drawn by four white horses. Her wedding ring had been made from Welsh gold, a royal family tradition since 1923.

Opposite above: The Queen, the Duchess of Cornwall and Carole Middleton pictured outside the Abbey.

Above: Time for the now-traditional kiss on the balcony.

Right above: The Family assemble on the balcony.

Right bottom: After the lunchtime reception, Prince William drives his new bride back to Clarence House in his father's Aston Martin. Decorated by Prince Harry the registration number reads 'JU5T WED'. A private reception, hosted by the Prince of Wales, followed that evening.

Celebrating the Duke's 90th Birthday

Right: The Duke pictured on his 90th birthday, 10 June 2011.

Below: The royal family gathered at Windsor for a service to mark the Duke's birthday on 12 June 2011.

Bottom: The Prime Minister David Cameron and his wife Samantha welcome the Queen and the Duke of Edinburgh to Downing Street for a celebratory lunch.

Zara Phillips Marries

Above: Zara Phillips married England rugby star Mike Tindall on 30 July 2011. The couple chose to have a private ceremony, held in the Canongate Kirk in Edinburgh, followed by a reception in the Palace of Holyroodhouse. Crowds gathered in force along the Royal Mile to watch members of the royal family arrive for their second wedding of the year.

Right: At the end of June William and Kate set off on their first official overseas tour. With the eyes of the world following them, they completed a highly successful eleven-day visit to Canada and the United States. Here they are special guests at a BAFTA event in Hollywood, after which *People* magazine said that Kate brought 'glamour, grace and star power' to the occasion.

Diamond Jubilee celebrations begin

Left: Braving inclement weather in April 2012, the Queen and the Duke of Edinburgh visit Greenland Dock in Greenwich, South London, to formally name the new Royal Rowbarge, *The Gloriana*. The 94-foot vessel, painstakingly built by master craftsmen, is ornately carved and covered in gold leaf. Powered by 18 oarsmen, it will head a pageant of more than 1,000 boats on the River Thames on 3 June 2012 to mark the Queen's Diamond Jubilee.

Below centre: As part of her Diamond Jubilee tour, the Queen and Prince Philip accept gifts and flowers from local school children during a walkabout in Windsor. Over 1,000 people turned out to give her a warm welcome in the town, where she also met local couples celebrating their 60th wedding anniversary during her Jubilee year.

Opposite and centre above right & left: Wearing a stunning lavender and baby blue bouclé tweed coat, Her Majesty the Queen is all smiles on a visit to Bromley in May, where she takes tea and cake with couples celebrating their 60th wedding anniversary in 2012.

Left: The Duchess of Cambridge accompanies the Queen to Leicester.

Above: Resplendent in scarlet, the Queen and the Duke attend a service for the Order of the British Empire at St Paul's Cathedral. The Queen is the Sovereign of the Order and the Duke of Edinburgh is Grand Master.

A flotilla of this size has not been seen on the Thames for over 350 years, when one sailed in honour of King Charles II's restoration of the monarchy.

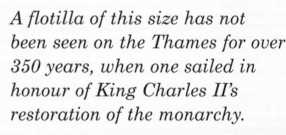

Pageant on the Thames

The Queen and other members of the royal family on board the Royal Barge, the *Spirit of Chartwell,* during the Diamond Jubilee Pageant on the Thames, 3 June 2012. Decorated with over 10,000 blooms, the barge formed the heart of the 1,000-strong flotilla which travelled between Battersea Bridge and Tower Bridge. Despite heavy rain, over one million people poured into central London to watch a spectacular display of river-craft of all shapes and sizes, paying tribute to Her Majesty the Queen. A flotilla of this size had not been seen on the Thames for over 350 years, when one sailed in honour of King Charles II's restoration of the monarchy.

The *Spirit of Chartwell* carried the Queen, the Duke of Edinburgh, the Prince of Wales, the Duchess of Cornwall, the Duke and Duchess of Cambridge and Prince Harry through the bascules of Tower Bridge where they disembarked to board *HMS President* to watch the flotilla pass by.

The Archbishop of Canterbury paid tribute to the Queen's lifelong dedication to her country and the Commonwealth.

Service of Thanksgiving

Top, left and opposite. The Queen attends a service of Thanksgiving at St Paul's Cathedral on 5 June without the Duke of Edinburgh, who was admitted to hospital the previous day for treatment of a bladder infection. During the service she is supported by the Prince of Wales. The seating arrangements were changed so that she would sit with Prince Charles rather than at the front on her own. The Archbishop of Canterbury offered words of support for the Duke and paid tribute to the Queen's lifelong dedication to her country and the Commonwealth.

Above: After the Thanksgiving Service the Queen sparkles at at a Mansion House reception, which she attended along with the other senior royals – the Prince of Wales, the Duchess of Cornwall, the Duke and Duchess of Cambridge and Prince Harry – hosted by the Lord Mayor of London, before travelling on to a lunch at Westminster Hall.

From the Balcony

Above and inset right: The Queen, accompanied by the Prince of Wales, the Duchess of Cornwall and the Duke and Duchess of Cambridge, waves to the enthusiastic crowds from the balcony at Buckingham Palace after returning from the Service of Thanksgiving at St Paul's Cathedral. The route back, after a lunch at Westminster Hall, was lined with flag-bearing crowds all trying to catch a glimpse of the royal party.

Opposite: The Red Arrows aerobatic team fly low in formation over Buckingham Palace, trailing red, white and blue plumes. The crowd's cheering is drowned out by the noise of the jets as they soar away over The Mall. The flypast began with a Lancaster bomber and four Spitfires followed by a Hurricane. It brought a spectacular end to the events of the Jubilee weekend.

Middle right: Prince Charles pays tribute to the Queen at the Diamond Jubilee Concert held in her honour outside Buckingham Palace on the evening of 4 June. Robbie Williams kicked off the event with 'Let Me Entertain You', backed by the Regimental Band of the Coldstream Guards, followed by a string of other stars including Tom Jones, Kylie Minogue, Sir Elton John and Sir Paul McCartney.

Bottom right: Kylie Minogue and Lee Thompson of Madness are introduced to the Queen after the concert.

Order of the Garter

Opposite: The Queen and Prince Philip lead the procession to the Order of the Garter Service at St George's Chapel, Windsor 18 June 2012. The most senior and oldest British Order of Chivalry, the Garter was founded in 1348 by Edward III. Membership is limited to those who have held public office and who have made a contribution to national life. Present royal members include the Queen as Sovereign of the Order, Prince Philip, the Prince of Wales, the Princess Royal and Princes Andrew, Edward and William. If there are new Companions of the Order, they are formally invested before the procession at Windsor Castle. After lunch, the Knights of the Garter process on foot to the service at St George's Chapel, wearing their velvet robes and hats with white plumes.

Opposite below: The Queen is joined by William and Kate on her Diamond Jubilee visit to Nottingham on 13 June 2012.

Left: The Queen and the Duke of Edinburgh arrive at Epsom Racecourse to watch The Derby along with 130,000 race-goers.

Above: The Queen on the second day of Royal Ascot, seen here greeting Princess Haya bint Al Hussein of Jordan.

Below: The Queen and Prince Philip arriving for Ladies' Day at Royal Ascot.

Opening the 2012 London Olympics

Top: A sudden downpour did not dampen the spirits of the Queen as she met with Olympic torch bearer Gina MacGregor and Lord Coe, Chairman of the London 2012 Organising Committe, in the grounds of Windsor Castle during the London Olympic 2012 Torch Relay.

Above: The Queen is the guest of honour at the opening ceremony of the London 2012 Olympics, where she officially opened the Games. Earlier in the evening, Her Majesty had stunned millions, including most of her close family, by appearing in a spoof James Bond film clip with Daniel Craig.

Left: Jacques Rogge, the President of the International Olympic Committee, speaking at a reception held by the Queen for members of the IOC at Buckingham Palace.

Right: A visit to the Olympic Park in July 2012.

Inset: Her Majesty attends the unveiling of the Bomber Command Memorial in Green Park, London, in June 2012. The memorial is dedicated to the 55,573 RAF crew who lost their lives in the Second World War. Following the dedication, thousands of poppies were released from the sky in tribute.

Below: The Royal party pictured in Scotland in August 2012. The Duke was admitted to Aberdeen Royal Infirmary while staying at Balmoral, just two months after he had spent five nights in hospital with a bladder infection following the Diamond Jubilee Pageant in June.

In Remembrance

Top: The Duke stops to talk to Chelsea Pensioners at the opening of the Royal British Legion's Field of Remembrance at Westminster Abbey in November 2012.

Above: The Queen pictured with Prime Minister David Cameron and Foreign Secretary William Hague at number 10 Downing Street. The Queen's visit to the weekly Cabinet meeting as an observer was the first time a monarch has attended the meeting since Queen Victoria's reign.

Left: In 2012 the Queen recorded her Christmas message in 3D for the first time. She paid tribute to Great Britain's Olympic and Paralympic athletes for inspiring the nation during a 'splendid summer of sport'.

Harry, like his brother William, increasingly shows the talents of his mother in connecting with people at all levels, making these brothers the new face of the British monarchy.

Top: The royal couple appear to be enjoying a visit to the Bank of England in December 2012.

Above inset: The Queen takes a moment to pet a horse as she meets members of the Household Cavalry at Combermere Barracks in Windsor in November 2012.

Left: Prince Harry explains some of the features of the the Sentebale Forget-me-not garden at the Chelsea Flower Show in May 2013. Sentebale, a charity founded by Prince Harry and Prince Seeiso of Lesotho, aims to help victims of poverty and Lesotho's HIV and AIDS epidemic.

Celebrating the Coronation

Top: Her Majesty is very much amused on the balcony following Trooping the Colour in June 2013. The Duke of Edinburgh was absent from the ceremony as he was recuperating from abdominal surgery.

Left and above: The Royal party files out of Westminster Abbey on 4 June during the celebrations of the 60th anniversary of the Coronation; the Dean of Westminster, Dr John Hall, talks to the Queen.

Opposite: The Queen is obviously delighted to present the Duke with the Order of New Zealand, the country's highest honour, at Buckingham Palace on 6 June.

Happy Events

Opposite above: Prince Andrew presents his delighted mother with the Gold Cup after her horse Estimate won the feature race at Royal Ascot on 20 June 2013.

Opposite below left: The Queen leaves the London Clinic after visiting Prince Philip on his 92nd birthday, 10 June.

Opposite below right: England cricketer Kevin Pietersen shakes hands with the Queen ahead of the first day of the second test between England and Australia at Lord's Cricket Ground on 18 July.

Right: The Duke and Duchess of Cambridge give the world its first glimpse of their firstborn, Prince George Alexander Louis, third in line to the throne of the United Kingdom, on the steps of St Mary's Hospital, London, on 23 July.

Below: The Queen and Duke of Edinburgh attend the 2014 Glasgow Commonwealth Games Baton relay launch ceremony at Buckingham Palace on 9 October 2013. After presenting the baton to the Queen, the relay continued its journey to visit all 70 competing nations and territories.

A New Heir

Prince George Alexander Louis Cambridge was christened in a formal ceremony at the Chapel Royal in St James's Palace on 23 October 2013, conducted by Archbishop of Canterbury Justin Welby, in the presence of the Queen and a select number of family and friends. While the location broke with a long tradition of Buckingham Palace baptisms, the infant Prince was dressed in an outfit made of intricate Honiton lace and white satin – identical to one worn by every baby born to the British Royal family since 1841 when Queen Victoria's eldest daughter was christened in the original.

At a champagne reception afterwards the close family posed for formal photographs in the Morning Room at Clarence House; these captured four generations and three heirs in-line to the throne photographed together.

Prince George's seven godparents included Zara Phillips (pictured above left with husband Mike Tindall) and a mix of contemporaries from school and university days but also older confidantes, Julia Samuel, once a close friend of Diana's and Jamie Lowther-Pinkerton who served for seven years as private secretary and equerry to William and Harry.

126

During these years as your Queen, the support of my family has, across the generations, been beyond measure. Prince Philip is, I believe, well-known for declining compliments of any kind. But throughout he has been a constant strength and guide.

Acknowledgements

The photographs in this book are from the archives of the *Daily Mail*.

Particular thanks to Alan Pinnock, Steve Torrington, Dave Sheppard,
Brian Jackson, and all the staff.

Thanks also to Gareth Thomas, Alison Gauntlett and Sarah Rickayzen,
Richard Betts and John Dunne.

This revised and updated edition published by Atlantic World in 2013

First published by Atlantic World as *Elizabeth: The Life and Reign of Elizabeth II* in 2012

Atlantic Publishing

38 Copthorne Road

Croxley Green

Hertfordshire

WD3 4AQ

Hardback ISBN 978-1-909242-38-8

Paperback ISBN 978-1-909242-39-5

Printed and bound in China